No Fresh Cut Flowers

An Afterlife Anthology

Other titles by Sephyrus Press:

Intuitive Art: How to Have a Two-Way Conversation with Your Higher Self, by Rachel Archelaus

Color Your Aura: An Aura & Chakra Coloring Book for Young Children, by Rachel Archelaus

Sappho Does Hay(na)ku, by Scott Keeney

52 Things, by Rachel Archelaus

No Fresh Cut Flowers

An Afterlife Anthology

Edited by,
Rachel Archelaus

Sephyrus Press
Phoenix

Copyright © 2010 by Sephyrus Press

All rights reserved

Second Edition Trade Paperback

No Fresh Cut Flowers, An Afterlife Anthology, edited by Rachel Archelaus

ISBN: 978-0-9830137-0-9

Book Design by Tina Mingolello
Typeset by Jocelyn Sedlor
Photographs by Rachel Archelaus

Sephyrus Press
www.sephyruspress.com

Dedication

This book is dedicated to the clouds for renewing my wonder every day.

Soundtrack

Six songs were created by various artists to accompany this book. Enjoy the full experience by downloading the soundtrack here: sephyrus.com/soundtrack.

Contents

Introduction / RACHEL ARCHELAUS	1
Earthly Obsession / CHANGMING YUAN	5
A Life's Conclusion / J.J. STEINFELD	7
Closed eyes no longer meaning sleep . . . / KAREN NEUBERG	9
Black Ice / ARIEL CHANCE DEVILLE	11
George Washington Bridge / RICHARD SCHIFFMAN	13
Changing of the Guard / RICHARD SCHIFFMAN	17
Grave talk / PHIL GRUIS	19
Flash Player / TOM CLARK	21
Reunion / BYRON DANZIGER	23
Asylum Wanderer / NICK DONIGER	25
All Hallow's E'en / PENN KEMP	27
Heaven Up Here / TOM CLARK	29
Hereafter / TONI CLARK	31
Kingdom Come / PHIL GRUIS	33
Flying / LAURY EGAN	35
My Mother's House / LAURY EGAN	37
Naming Afterlife / J.J. STEINFELD	41
No Fresh Cut Flowers on Cow Parsley Corner / P. A. LEVY	43
Oh Yes / SCOTT KEENEY	45
Over the Marsh and Far Away / PENN KEMP	49

Physics / GARY BECK	51
Prayer of a Displaced Soul / CJ CLAYTON DIPPOLITO	53
Roadkill Revenge / PHIL GRUIS	55
Sentry / AYARA STEIN	59
September 24 / BARBARA BIALICK	61
Sex After Death / LISKEN VAN PELT DUS	63
Song for Maud / ANNA TABORSKA	65
Sun's in the West / MARY BELARDI ERICKSON	67
Text Valentine / PETER RENNICK	69
Collision Valentine / PETER RENNICK	71
A Postmortem Assignment for O'Keeffe / RICHARD SCHIFFMAN	73
The Garden in Her Own Mind / RICHARD SCHIFFMAN	75
The Other Side of the Grave / AYARA STEIN	77
Collision / SCOTT KEENEY	79
The Shadow of Love Cast on a New Day / P. A. LEVY	81
The Vodou Afterlife / GRETA BOLGER	83
Fragment from The Dog Sutra / LYNN HOFFMAN	85
Threshold / LAURY EGAN	87
Weather Report from Heaven / NEIL ELLMAN	89
CONTRIBUTOR NOTES	91
ACKNOWLEDGMENTS	99

No Fresh Cut Flowers

An Afterlife Anthology

Introduction

I was twelve years old when my Grandfather died.

During dinner one night the phone rang. My Dad got up and answered it, listened for a few moments, then ran up the stairs sobbing. I don't remember the rest of that day. I think I was paralyzed because I'd never seen my Father cry before.

I went to school the next day and handed in my homework to my Science teacher and mentioned what had happened the night before. He was surprised I'd come to school, everyone was. I didn't really understand why it was so strange, sure I felt a little sadness but since my Grandpa had moved to Florida a few years earlier it wasn't much of a shock to my everyday life not to have him around.

I believe it was three days after he died when he made his first visit. He looked like he always had, his stocky body dressed in fine clothing. I recognized this display as him but he wasn't a solid figure. The door, desk and candles he was standing in front of were still visible through his button-down shirt. He spoke to me and I heard it but not through my ears. It was in my head. Sort of a mixture of his tone and vocabulary in my voice. I got out of the bed and hugged the air where he stood and finally, I cried.

That was the beginning of my double life. A world atop the corporeal one we all know was set upon me and kept expanding each year. Soon I could see auras and feel the emotions of others. Life as a teenager was trying enough without the distraction of hearing the thoughts of my peers and being pestered by ghosts. Driving was difficult as spirits have no fear of being run over and tend to cross the road in front of oncoming traffic. Most people wouldn't notice this, but to me it evoked the same reaction as it would be to drive knowingly into a crossing child.

It took many years to learn how to control these new senses but as it happened life became sweeter. It gave me the opportunity to view death in a whole new light. These friends and relatives were not really gone, they had just transformed beyond the physical. I learned they were available for chats when I missed them most and that I could reunite my family with their lost loved ones as well. The finest example I have is when I saw my Grandmother for the first time after she'd passed. She was ill with emphysema for many years and could barely walk through a department store without the need for oxygen. The first time I saw her after the funeral, she ran through my living room, happy as a clam, obviously well and with a huge smile on her face. There was such an ease about her, unlike anything I had seen on her face for years. They do this so we can heal. So we can feel alright about where they are and so we can let go of any guilt we've hung onto about our time with them.

For a short time this ability was my livelihood. I worked at a metaphysical center in New Milford, CT and acted as a translator for strangers and those they wished to contact. I also gave workshops and talks on the topics of psychic development and mediumship. I do believe we are all born with this connection intact. We lose it for a variety of reasons, the simplest one being that it's not encouraged. We acknowledge the existence of energy as it serves us in a physical way; to power our laptops and refrigerators. We can picture a buzzing yellow surge traveling through wires. Energy is much more subtle than that if we wish to see it. It resembles something more like cigar smoke or television fuzz. This is normally how spirits will show themselves, as my grandfather did the day he appeared in my bedroom.

There is no better way to play with the subtleties and varied perspectives of the afterlife theme than with poetry. Poets can morph language into seemingly tangible moments of consciousness, much like the moment of death. After receiving the submissions and narrowing them down into a multifaceted compilation it occurred to me that musicians also know how to transform energy into being. These musicians generously took inspiration from the poems and general theme producing an inspiring and thoughtful soundtrack to accompany the book.

What these artists have done individually is convey their own reality's eye on the afterlife. Combined, they swirl about into one whole idea. Not everyone believes there is an existence after our final moment on earth while others feel deeply that we continue to return to live life after life. I've enjoyed immensely diving into each piece and however abstract it may be, to live in their world for a time. Let this be an opportunity to live beyond your own world, if only for the time it takes to read a poem.

—Rachel Archelaus, editor

Earthly Obsession

in my forelife i was a caterpillar
moiling, toiling deep in the soil
hoping to be reincarnated someday
holding my head high above the earth

but the more i try to live like my fellow creatures
the less i can stop being a chrysalis
caged in a tiny and compact cocoon
cobwebbed with a stubborn and endless thread

i don't know if there will be an afterlife
now and here is all i am
without the sharpened knife of godly wisdom
can i hope to fly like a butterfly?

A Life's Conclusion

It is almost lunchtime
when the young nurse
tells you not to wander too far
you joke with her
that you have forfeited none of your appetite
for food or mischief
and your dreams, well, you didn't want to make her blush
you never believed that you would be so old
and she promises to listen to your dreams
tomorrow, and walks away sensually, you think
as you walk away also
and stumble upon a sketchbook
with clown faces and amusing animals
a child's depictions you decide
then the startling map
leading directly to the graveyard
where your parents are buried
discarding appointments and medication
you walk for ten days and ten nights
to the faraway cemetery
no fatigue, no hunger, no desire
for escape or sleep
only the relentless walking
until your arrival, sketchbook in hand
before you reach the gravesite
you see a flower on the grave of a stranger
a flower from another clime and time

growing deviously
and hear so many voices
that naming is impossible
but before the rationalization
and terrifying explanations and excuses
you hear all the disappointments
of your life and maybe a few
discarded dreams and experiences
and a single beautiful voice
declares, welcome home, lost child.

Closed eyes no longer meaning sleep...

Beside me, destiny,
mid-wrap, is hesitating

while I envision my ancestors
preparing the feast.

Everyone welcome includes
wistful faces once glimpsed

in crumbling photographs.
One of them sure to serve

honey cake, another apple pie.
We will discuss whether

enough wind will arrive
to turn the millers windmill,

or to billow sails across
the doldrums.

A ballet of children
tiptoe in the steam

rising in the winds
of centuries. A thousand

mothering hands
reach to hold

again. This
is the feast that occurs

when someone
in the chain of family

dies. Everyone comes
to greet them, to tell

them their part
in the story.

There is no time
measured at the table.

It is always beginning,
and there is always enough.

Black Ice

She lifts
the hem of her slip
like black ice,
soft-eyed residence
of slick demise,
blackest eyes
entreating,
black black pupils beating,
eating into resistance;
entrancing,
enchanting,
holding up
the gates of some strange paradise
with a pistol in each hand.

Mythic creature of vengeance,
she,
guardian of the portal
to some bleak
afterlife: a moment,
a moment of pleasure
passing;
a breath of air,
a taste of all that is holy.

And she
lifts the hem of her
slip like black
ice.

George Washington Bridge

This morning, spied through morning's eyes,
the bridge, my scalloped neighbor
to the north, appeared a tinker-toy
construction, the cars and trucks and buses—
crawling east, crawling west—
between the Palisades and the Heights
were also toys, the river sequined,
the river boats were galleons, the sky
a blue balloon, the bridge a plaited hammock
strung between two boughs.

But then the clouds came twirling in like tops,
and the wind too struck up its fiddles soughing
the glass towers, the blue balloon flown far away.
The bridge, the bridge now lost in mists.
How very quickly all is changed.

In Nepal there are rope bridges flung across
the abyss. When long ago I crossed one—
it creaked and swayed. How many sherpas
fully loaded—heading east, heading west—
before the straw rope frays,
before the frayed rope snaps?

All things we make will be unmade.
The span outside my window,
not lashed of jungle vines,
but stitched of twisted steel,
has stood three quarters of a century.

Today the cables are madly pinging.
Still, this engineering marvel will not soon fold.
More stable than the minds that made it,
unshaken as the bluffs it tethers—
arching like a cat. The cat is hissing.
The cat is bounding. The cat has got
nine more lives to live.

But what about me? What tethers me
to this sole life? And after vaulting
the chasm of the years, will I too land
on padded feet? Or is life's leap all—
untethered, heading neither east
nor west—bridge that bridges
nothing to itself?

The storm soon passed
that seethed the heart's wild river,
which lies now like a lamb, no longer a lion,
nor even a cat hissing. And the galleons
return to ply, the bridge lights glinting
in the dusk in which doubt is impossible.
It cannot live at night
when nothing is known,
or needs to be.

Therefore, I speak of bridges—
how seamlessly they bind shore to unseen shore,
though they themselves are temporal
and flung though space.

The night is a bridge between two days.
A rainbow bridges the mountain to the plains.
Thought spans the gap between silences.
Love too—a prey to storms and violent churnings—
that frailest bridge of all binding solitude to solitude
across a pathlessness of air. And even death
I'm guessing is a bridge to somewhere—

We'll find out where.

Changing of the Guard

The living hold onto pieces of the dead—
one has got my mother's shambling gait,
another her time-splotched hands, still others
her sunken, sallow cheeks, her aluminum walker,
her melancholy smile. I pass them on the street,
and in the subway. They walk by the diner
window as I eat. Like autumn leaves,
the dead swirl past in bits and drabs.
Or they flail at us with tentacles that don't quite hold,
as mermaids lunged at passing sailors.
But with the years these visitations dwindle.
Whatever they keep of the dead,
the living gradually release it: hobbling
off on their own walkers, they let my mother
leave her brave and battered life behind.

Grave talk

A dark wind swerves around tombstones,
surges between iron pickets,
assailing him
with the great dense murmur
of the terminally
resigned

whose voices
drone endlessly on ...

TV   money   football
cholesterol   pills   the weather
(wait five minutes and it'll change haha)
shoes   hair   power tools   TV.

Or they grouse about politics
with no less result
than when they lived.

He claps hands over ears
and sprints across the street
into the safe glow
of yellow houselights
and blue windows

where forks and canned laughter clatter
and forgettable music weaves
through the babble of voices
droning endlessly on.

One side of Elm Street
isn't far from the other.

Flash Player

Strange to turn to old ghosts, watch ourselves dissolve
In their eyes. They were not here to help us,
Merely to drag us back against our will
Into a dim becalmed past, then forward into
Occluded presents which yet feel too bright

Reunion

We arrived in a new place
Greeted at the gate
We passed through
Not knowing what to expect

Non-existent speech
Communicating by other means
Body and mind are useless
A gathering of a different sort

Coming to realize
We cannot be seen
Trying to find ourselves
Lost in a union of souls

Hoping that some being will sing
Or some being will speak
But the silence is deafening
And we are briefly lost ...

No substance left
Yet we are content
Just to be harmonic souls
In a new existence

Sense the hope of all
To mourn a previous existence
Silly, sad, and true
But regret is of no consequence

Free of our former domains
Breaking from our shells
Metamorphic
Until the universe engulfs us

One with the cosmic energy
Part of an ancient gathering
Forces balancing life
And what is beyond . . .

Asylum Wanderer

On a rock
Under the shade of a looming pine
At the start of the path
To the high meadow
I sit and watch
Those who do not see me
Their ancestors
Caused me to suffer.
In tunnels and lairs
Bellow massive brick structures
I felt the wrath
Of misguided treatments.
My sensitivity to sudden light
Was a mild condition.
When they saw me
Fall to the floor
Convulsing,
Eyes rolled back,
I was sent here.
I was sent to my death.
Now I sit and watch
Those who do not see me.
Their fathers
Caused me to suffer.
At night, I float down the hills
And cry out to this town

Never expecting reply
Or validation
Or apology
For what it has taken from me.

All Hallow's E'en

All day I have made ready
celebrating one more fall
of leaves, celebrating

the sky, blue against orange
maple. Feeling transition, just
as the sky widens to receive you.

The stars embrace your ascent
on Samhain, fire festival, when
a wheel of planets sings you free.
Trick or Treat. Shell out, shell out.

In late evening I stroll by the river
through woods not dark but lit so
ghostly by borrowed light pollution

spread like fog. I meditate on limestone
blocks left by Bobcat's last improvement.
The creek ripples by, reflecting light.

Behind me, a tree shakes. A form emerges
out of stillness, solidifies into familiar
silhouette. A presence, strong and still.

You are with me. A buck rubs his antler
against the maple, shearing his pain away.
A rack of three tines, fully mature.

I've never seen a deer around here.
He freezes as I turn round, stock still
while we regard one another. When

at last I rise, his silhouette dissolves
with the white flag of his tail. His musk
fills the glen. His presence lingers.

What has called you back? This is
your home, your domain after dark
on the only night when you might return,

regarding with furrowed brow the skin you
shed, rubbing against rough bark the sore
velvet of new antlers. You belong here.

These woods are neither dark nor deep.
They're the fringe of floodplain by the creek.
You have no more miles before you sleep.

Heaven Up Here

Beyond nostalgia
And expectation all life
A process
Of removal from life
Translation

Into whatever's out there
Or isn't
Air or aether
Entering celestial clouds
In the moment of liftoff

A light feathery moment
In which
To depart is to arrive

Violet shadows glow
As if filled with nutrient
Of the afterlife

Blue avenues of ozone
Blank atonal diffused
Through the reflected square
Of sunlight
On the floor beyond the waiting
Room chair

Wouldn't it be nice
Like leaving the room
Without leaving your chair

Though I haven't yet been convinced
I'll be so gently
Hurled
Into that floating world

Hereafter

I'm going to live online when I get old.
I hope the nursing homes all have high-speed
connections, wireless Internet, e-mail
with good spam-blockers, and RSS feed.
At last, I'll have uninterrupted hours
to read the boards, to roam the blogosphere—
a password as my passport, an ID
for every portal in the new frontier.
And this is all the immortality
I ask for: On the far side of the screen,
I'll leave my electronic fingerprints
so that at last, part of me might, unseen,
slip through some cyber-door that's left ajar
and live forever through my avatar.

Kingdom come

Downtown in choking grit and fumes
a black-clad man thrusts into my hand
a flimsy leaflet, invitation to
   Life in a Peaceful
      New World

where golden leaves frame
snowy peaks, bountiful fields and forests,
tidy houses discrete on a pristine lake.

A laughing boy,
his basket full of cheeky apples,
watches mother and child pet a bear,
feed it purple berries.

Down the grassy slope
dad lifts daughter
to stroke a lion's mane.

Families in this New World
are nuclear and prosperous.
No one toils without reward.
Hosannas ring in the crystal air.

Everyone is smooth of brow,
broadly smiling, at ease
head to toe
in loose clothing
and vague ethnicity

cheered by plentitude –
and by dearth.

No crime. No slums. No dope.
No pierced queers or sk8tr boyz.
No war. No death.
No pain, no tears.

No Linda,
ruby pendant
wild between her breasts.

Flying

Flying, skin shed, without division
from the wind exhaling into all spaces:
filling square-rigged sails of ships below,
ghostly galleons, bowsprits proud.

Flying, slow spirals, free from the worry
of our own weightiness, freightless and
unattached, with no intent, to no port.

Flying, unfocused as the vaguest clouds,
passing over cities, rivers, and oceans,
unconcerned with the violent blares
of yellow lightning or the booming
doomsday voice of thunder.

Flying through any open window,
without following lanes or streets
or guiding lights, held to no measurement
or schedule, not needing the safety
of harbors, not worrying about
the towering reach of rogue waves.

Flying, like colorless fireworks
eternally falling, seeing all, laughing
at the humor of the resounding universe
and that being whom the fearful call God,
who died as all do, sublimely oblivious
to man's beseeching cries, no more,
no less a creator than I.

My Mother's House

When I'm about to list my mother's house
    her maids arrive
    didn't know she'd died
    they sit down in living room chairs
    and cry
    brooms and mops beside them
    then they wipe their eyes
    and disappear.

Soon after
my mother comes
    perhaps because it's cleaning day
    old habits die hard
    even for the dead.

As my mother and I walk the house
    rooms condense and tip
    wide pine floors
    telescope through doors
    to touch brown-beamed ceilings.

Sometimes she is absent
    dissolves into plaster walls stained
    from years of cigarette and fireplace smoke
    shrouds of death and dust
    the colorlessness of dreams.

Sometimes she is present
    her face a chalk sketch on black paper
        posterized
            half positive
                half negative.

At last I confess
I don't wish to keep the house
    it holds its denizens too tight
        clutching the alive and dead alike
            its only view is of itself.

My mother is upset
    wants her red-and-white coffee cup
        her ceramic ashtray and pink pjs
            her kitchen where she used to sit
            playing solitaire
                the old dog's hair
            on the blue loveseat.

As dust motes rise in the dreary light
    she blends into shadows
        from somewhere
        I hear the realtor knock
            guilt quakes my heart.

How can I sell my mother's house?

I wander through the rooms
    up and down stairs leading nowhere
        through collapsing walls
        to heat-seared attics
            chilly earthen crawlspaces
                searching
                for the realtor
                and my mother.

I wake
    shot from the black enclave of sleep
    into the violent glare of sun
        morning birdsong cannot cancel
        the sadness of eleven years
            or erase my loss of her
            and her loss of this house.

Naming Afterlife

What happens if there really is
a geographical Hell
and a geographical Heaven
and there you are
your last thought, nothing momentous,
and your last breath, slightly musical,
and if you were really clever
and somewhat sentient
your memorable last words
behind you, left to the living
to contemplate and reassess
and somehow in an incorporeal
contradictory egocentric manner
manage to shake your head
or the memory of your head
because despite all the commotion
and luscious symbolism before you
you don't know which is which
geographical Hell or geographical Heaven
and the etiquette of the place
where you assume in a wishy-washy
imprecise former way-of-life thinking
you will be spending all of timelessness
with more souls than you could count
in a million irrational lifetimes
these myriad souls who wouldn't have given

you the time of day if you had passed on the street
and now won't even tell you the name of your residence
so you look for a familiar historical face
in that incorporeal contradictory manner
say a historically recognized saintly figure
or a historically recognized despotic figure
and then, if logic is anything like your life before
you'll finally know where you are

No Fresh Cut Flowers on Cow Parsley Corner

Norman towers like flint faced castles
guard a crop of rotting headstones
that lie deep in the overgrown garden
                       of the forgotten.
Canterbury bells peel out purple chimes
to names from the past
            decorated with ivy,
                      protected by nettles,
coloured forget-me-not blue.
And as whispers of serenity
                    calm echoes of sobs
footsteps are hushed by rye grass
and by moss.

Finding our spot I lean back against: 'Charlotte,
our beloved',
    then much missed,
                  now abandoned
to dandelion tales under a lichen stained blanket.
You spread out a tartan rug, place set our picnic,
all alone, we three gossip
in cow parsley corner.
Nibble cheese and cucumber sandwiches, sip tea,
pick poppies and buttercups for Charlotte,
                     'sadly taken from us',
             August 1865 aged only thirteen.

Shackled in daisy chains
                underneath
             the yew tree
we're willing prisoners in this afternoon idyll,
wondering how poor Charlotte died,
some nasty plague so we decide;
    ring-a-ring o' roses,
        ah-tishoo!
                ah-tishoo!
                        Charlotte fell down.

We three laughed,
                meadow laughs,
until the tiring sun said it was time for his bed,
and as we packed-up and said our farewells
the wind,
   a soft summer breeze,
cried like a beautiful voice at prayer.
It was just then,
   as I was staring into your eyes,
I noticed, in reflection,
                        a lost cloud drift by.

Oh Yes

Yesterday I died.
It was my third and final time.

At least at last
there is no more
falling leaves
hostility.

I should have been a pair of retractable claws
clicking across the hardwood floors
of quiet living rooms.

Death fit around me
like a brand new sock.

Over-the-calf,
tube,
the way life entered:

I in
you, I in
you, I in you.

No idea what to do
with myself now.

All of the people I loved
are here except
of course the ones down
there.

Only there is no up,
no down. No here here.

I saw you standing on our maple tree
on the lowest branch
no human can reach
and you were smiling
not remembering that I was gone.

"Good times, good times."

A fatal belief in things
coming together.

Cartoons shout Hooray
therefore I was
OK with my children watching
them in moderation.

The white breath of waiting
for the bus
against the multi-colored leaves
in late October . . .

where I would have been
today.

As a century is
something only thought of.

Yesterday I died.
My daughter climbed our tree
three years from now.

Over the Marsh and Far Away

She scries how to float above a body left behind.
Her route is through the Bardo and beyond.

Back in the realm of time we have just
habit to fall back on, the familiar wet

clothes that suit us to a thread worn
and weary with mourning. Hair pulled

out by the root. If only. Only if. Faith
less. Faith full. We don't know which.
She has chosen. Nor why. But words

over the abyss, one by one, a phrase or
sentence, lead us out of the bog, lead us home.

And on the way, perched on the word, we bend
to pick blueberries, sprigs of Labrador tea, scarlet

cranberry: bog fruit found and offered freely
to whatever guides are willing to hold her flame.

Grief is no time for emotion. The sky opens
and opens unto more sky. Lighter and lighter.

She rises. Nothing can bog her down now
she is ageless, genderless, free from teenage girl
angst. While we age more with each moment,
caught in cultural specifics that label us she, he,
confined to the particularities of person and of loss.

Physics

So much then
of this careless youth
spent in fleeting moments
that are briefly lent
to use with care, or thrift
and then the swift decline
in which we fall
blazing bits of matter
churning the vast universe
for an instant of combustion
then dispersed into primal gas.

Prayer of a Displaced Soul

I lay in this womb too silent,
remembering a radiance so bright,
it pains my crumbled heart to think of it.
Sinking hands in a tide pool,
grasping at silversides, a sea-salted kiss.

I float in the reminiscence,
feeding on what was.
Time has bound me
in the ethereal gauze of memory.

—How long 'til I awaken?
The ferryman's been paid
and my skull, bleached with two holes,
aches to behold the light again.
It is so dark, even the faintest of gloaming
would be something.

Baptize me in the wellspring,
set me down in the garden.
I plead for Creation to find me,
hidden in my quiet sarcophagus.

Roadkill revenge

The road shot in –
   an asphalt blast
   splintering great trees
   into toothpicks,
   pulverizing them for waste
   paper.

Years of cannonball cars
   hurtled rudely
   down gray highway...
   thunderous trucks
   transporting crap,
   spewing toxins,
   turning beast to grease.

Enough!

Tonight by the road
   dead 'coons rise.
   Deer reassemble themselves,
   bleached bones clicking.

Birds flail
   with crumpled wings
   in colliding clouds
   of desiccated bugs.

Flat cats reinflate.
   Sparky barks again.

Wilbur the old drunk
   is back on his feet.

Miranda pushes
   her bent bicycle,
   helmet askew
   on a fleshless skull.

A broken crowd
   staggers north,
   worms lagging.

As spirits rise
   numbers grow.
   As numbers grow
   spirits rise.
   Keening turns
   to angry growls,
   urgent moans
   and birdly twitters.

Ravens applaud
   with raucous caws
   this tattered parade
   shambling
   to a cruel S-curve

where with darkish glee
paws and wings,
hooves and hands
trundle tree trunks
onto the road

then join to beseech
the cackling night –
    O send us a Peterbilt,
    a herd of fleet Mustangs.

Sentry

Our island was a town of thin alleys
skirting the backs of neighbor's houses,
that became the undercover routes for me
and my boyfriend as we slunk through shadow,
jittery, and ready for the answers
to the mysteries. Death, what would it be like?
Was there really a heaven or a hell?
There was the question of sex, and then
what happened afterward. Each question gave
rise to another. Were our fates determined?
Was it a sin to kill? Did eternity
mean forever? As children, angelic
protection was given. A sentry
was assigned to each of us, and I pictured
a host hovering above, diaphanous,
intangible in their bright surveillance.
When Auntie died, they told me she'd become
my own special angel, watching me.
I loved to see her, brilliant redeemer —
nothing like she was when she was with us.
One night my boyfriend and I planned to do more
serious business than just kiss one night
or look at a sky with more stars than anywhere.
We stole a boat to get away from the rats and crabs.
So when light broke the first Wednesday of May
I cried when she saw me in that old boat,

swaying under a windswept pewter sky
losing my virginity at age sixteen,
not knowing why. I knew she saw it all,
and wondered why from floating Nirvana
she never once told me what I should do.
For all her resplendent wings full of wisdom,
she still remained as dumb and blind as I.
I understood why angels are endangered.
Struck by the sudden calm, we watched the sky
and couldn't bear to touch one another.
He cried, too, which scared me. So I left him,
and slipped overboard into the ocean.
He whispered my name across the waves
but I wouldn't answer; I don't know why.
Our parents waited for us in their homes,
wondered what had gone wrong with their children,
recalled how sweet we'd once been, how innocent,
the moment they first held us in their arms.

September 24

In the back of the local Starbucks,
where dark brown and chromium
yellow paint met in the middle of the wall,
there used to be one mahogany color table
and chair in the half-light hallway
that led to the men's and ladies rooms.

That's where the legend used to sit, sipping
free coffee as he busily scratched white
apocalyptic prose and complex patterns
or cartoons of himself on black boards.
He often gave away or sold these scratch-boards
or pink and yellow polka dot paintings like
the ones he got into the Museum of Bad Art…

When I last saw him, he was standing outside
the usual café, looking terribly thin with
shocking yellow eyes, and still smoking a cigarette.
"Can I get you a drink?" I asked him, but no,
he replied, "I've had enough drinks",
so we just stared fearfully at each other,
knowing we'd never meet again this life.
Then I walked away.

But that wasn't actually the last time I saw him.
Shortly after he died, I was at Starbucks,
hunched over a burgundy notebook,
trying to write poetry.
Just then I felt and saw a transparent arc
of energy hovering in front of me.
I knew it was him, my old acquaintance
And sad ghost, who couldn't let go
of his place. I wrote to him in my notebook:
    Goodbye, Sandy, You've got to leave now.

Today as I write this, a year later,
that same dark wood table is now standing
in the sunny middle of the front of the room,
next to mine, with no chair, and no artist, among a jumble
of us folks drinking coffee or working on computers,
at light pine-color furniture.
Is this an accidental memorial to the artist?
In its old space is now a brown
baby table, ready for a reincarnation.

Sex After Death

The ghosts arrive slowly, not
out of decorum but with attention

to presence, as if it is difficult
to remember. When they join me,

they are neither sitting nor standing.
I can't make out features, only

the landscape each ghost brings with it –
cold wildwater, tangled junglegreen,

pocked lavafield – all present with me,
here at the verge of sleep, death,

simultaneous lives, some kind
of pendulous truth endlessly

swinging. I light a fire
and it illuminates only my own face.

Nothing of the darkness is revealed.
The ghosts enter me, one after the other:

Waves, and a ship slicing through.
Heather and yellow rapeseed.

Mountain bursting into sky.
The fog we climbed through.

Song for Maud

Crows perch on my body
just as flowers grow on yours
spiders crawl on my face
like the breeze caresses yours

you lie in a meadow
I lie in a ditch
even in death I cannot touch you
even in death you flee my love

deer nuzzle your fingers
dogs chew at my bones
your voice was not for my ears
your gaze not for my face

the first kiss that I gave you
the last you ever felt

Sun's in the West

In the deepening light
thoughts drop into water
your mind rippling.

The sky a haze of blues,
 a loon calls
"Where from? Where to?"

You imagine going
entering worlds
you trust within
your touch
being.

You envision understanding
knowing you can sail beyond
necessity of docks

where you row
waves of infinity
lapping, forever lapping

in crisp sounds
across dusk's water.

Text Valentine

The lake-effect
love can have
on warm fronts
nature is dying
because she has
better things to do
always that piece
of trying to impress
someone lingers
lost migration
routes open up
icy mornings
nomads appear
still breathing
the afterlife.

Collision Valentine

Thinking backwards
finally you come to the city
where you ran out
of moon ran out of self
at the end of alone
covered with ants
you stopped to writhe
of a million irritations
you unburdened me
you fixed stars but
who does the thinking
when you come to the end
of matter the end
of antlers frozen
in the high beams?

A Postmortem Assignment
For Georgia O'Keeffe

Some things are hard like a bone,
the last flinty stone of life
glinting whiter than the noonday sun—
this pelvis bone of elk, humped
and notched, double socketed with air,
sickling cleanly through
the blue butter of forever.

Some things are soft like this satiny sky,
vacuous, vaporous, azure nothingness
timeless, placeless bucket of space,
through which the bright blade of this world
plows its prow in eternity's ocean.

But this hard thing, this narrow now,
this slivered moment honed thinner
than a bone—just here, just now—everything
we know, or can know, this palpable present,
this glinting scimitar sweeping through
stranger seas than we suspect

only appears hard, and this soft thing,
this paisley, pillowy hump of sky, this silky
smooth eternity, pearled with rafts of
cloud, this airy no-thing—for which we
have no name—through which all lives
are endlessly passing

only appears soft: hard and soft being
not just relative, but altogether meaningless
in a world where mind and matter, where here
and hereafter are inseparable—like the alternately
mortal and immortal twins Castor and
Pollux—dancing across another sky.

I'm talking about the sky within,
the sky which will still be there
after the hard bone of this body,
after the hard bone of this world
dissolve like the salt doll

which dove into the sea
to measure the sea's depth, and never
came up again to tell what it had found.
That salt doll is your self. Trust me, Georgia,
it is long gone, but somewhere
the incorruptible bone of it remains.
Your assignment is to paint that bone.

The Garden in Her Own Mind

When the doors to the world
slammed shut
she entered the garden,
when she could no longer walk
she knelt in the dirt,
when her muscles atrophied
she planted bulbs,
when she lost a husband
she mulched the bougainvillea,
in the winter of her life
she pored over seed catalogues,
when her children left
she lavished herself on roses,
as her lungs collapsed
she sniffed lilacs,
when her friends stopped calling
she called on an azalea.
This is how she lived,
this is how she moved
in the ever-narrowing gyre
of the garden,
eventually retreating
all the way to the calyx,
then the bud, the sprout, the seed.
And then we didn't see her.
And then we forget her.

And then she forgot herself.
But the garden remembered,
which she herself had planted,
the garden in her own mind.
Where she rests now
like burlaped root stock
in the interregnum
between life and life.

The Other Side of the Grave

Rain drips from the tolerant leaves of the sycamores.
Uptown: in front of the video store
a group of schoolgirls skitters by;
their bright laughter makes me want to love again.
These things I will remember forever
because they are matters of consequence.

Fear was the underside of every leaf
I turned, smacked with rain-scented kisses.
Knowing their very nests are made of music,
songbirds white as salt slide down
the polished rays of July sun and fan
ripples across the surface of the lake.
A world of sun and water
turned to shadows on a yellow page.

Darkness echoes in every cold shadow;
our own darkness trails us to the gate
among rashes and splashes of goldenrod
where a boy throws an orange to a girl
and she catches it.

Collision

When I die
Will you marry me?

The Shadow of Love Cast on a New Day

an unclaimed shadow falls in love
with the girl
      that tends
         the sun
    who cleans
        and sweeps
               the rays
            and polishes
         the light
            that illuminates youth

     so begins the history of happiness

            a reflection of her
                        collects colours
                  with rainbow chasers
            and
                  galavants
                        in the night sky
                              like a twinkle
                                    of a twinkle
                                          picking up
                                                diamonds
                                                      fallen loose
                                                            from lost stars

morning

                        strokes her
                              golden head
                  so full of heavenly fragments and spectrum glints
                                          all glitter spun
                              into celestial dusted thread
                                    that she weaves
                        the waft and the weft
                              into a bright
                                    new day

The Vodou Afterlife

If we believed, as NPR says the Haitians do,
in 16 reincarnations, half as men,
half as women, with a year and a day
in "the water" between each,
we could live for 800 years,

give or take, with a different body
each time, so that even when earthquakes
come, and hurricanes, and heart attacks,
even when help is hard to come by,
there is always next time, another chance

to hear what the rocks say, sense how the trees feel,
to learn again what the animals know.
Vodouisants are smart enough to know
that their big guy god, Bondye, is far distant
from creation, and cannot be held accountable,

so they send their prayers to the loa,
lesser spirits, like Papa Legba,
the guardian of the crossroads,
Erzulie Freda, the spirit of love, Simbi,
the spirit of rain and magicians,

Guede, the guardian of death.
They don't stick pins, not anymore, but
make fake people out of discarded shoes
and nail them on trees near the cemetery,
messengers to the otherworld, to say hello,

maybe, or help us out with these hurricanes, or
send us some rain in this unbreathable heat, or
give us strong magic, or to scream enough with
the crossroads already, we're already dead.
Send water, Erzulie Freda. Send shovels.

Fragment from The Dog Sutra

Bill the Dog said:
Oh compassionate, playful, peace-seeking Buddha,
why do we care for human touch?

And the Blue Dog Buddha, whose every breath
is a snort of joy and compassion barked
to shatter the bonds of blindness and said:

Every dog who is stroked one million times by a human being
gets true release and rebirth in the pure land in which there is no suffering.
A human who strokes a dog one million times
gets rebirth ten times greater than the one he left.
A human who strokes a second dog one million times
gets a rebirth one hundred times better than the one she left.
A human who strokes three dogs one million times a dog,
gets reborn as a dog.
And from there, The Great Vanishing is just a million strokes away.

Threshold

Black triangular shadow
angles from door frame, points
to an interior, a déjà vu invitation.

I hesitate to cross the threshold.

Stepping inside will strop old sorrows,
whet their ability to inflict fresh wounds.

Yet I am compelled to enter.

The room is light with pale colors
but saturated with accumulated sadness.

My parents wait.

Are they ghosts or fictions of imagination?
Under terms of dreams they could be either.

We speak.

But all we never said, now will never
pass our lips: love hovers unexpressed.

They beg for things I can't give.

How do I explain they've lost life
and the ability to possess?

In silence, I grieve.

And then, dissatisfied with
the limitations of my dream plot
or harkened to their otherworldly address,
slowly they dissolve into nothingness.

Weather Report from Heaven

We get used to the seasons
When alive
Heat and cold
Leaves falling from the trees
And born again in spring
But here it's all the same
Day in, day out:
The barometer stands still
Fair with a gentle breeze
Some wispy clouds
(Or are they angel wings?)
No rain, no snow—
My prayer is simply this:
Oh Lord,
I'd rather be in Philadelphia.

Contributor Notes

Penn Kemp: Poet, performer and playwright Penn Kemp has published twenty-five books of poetry and drama, had six plays and ten CDs produced as well as a DVD and several award-winning videopoems. She performs in festivals around the world. Penn is currently Writer-in-Residence at University of Western Ontario. She hosts an eclectic literary show, Gathering Voices, on CHRWradio.com/talk/gatheringvoices. She is a Leo with a mane of hair that will outlast her!

Byron Danziger is 38 years old and lives in Naugatuck, CT. His first letter written was the letter B and it has been an uphill battle ever since. This is his first time published. He was named after the poet, Lord Byron. We will await with much anticipation the future works of Byron Danziger.

P.A. Levy: Born in East London but now residing amongst the hedge mumblers of rural Suffolk, P.A.Levy has been published in many magazines, both on line and in print, from 'A Cappella Zoo' to 'Zygote In My Coffee' and many places in-between. He is also a founding member of the Clueless Collective and can be found loitering on page corners and wearing hoodies at www.cluelesscollective.co.uk

Richard Schiffman splits his time between New York City and an adobe cabin in the mountains of northern New Mexico. He has written two spiritual biographies: "Mother of All—A Revelation of the Motherhood of God in the Life and Teachings of the Jillellamudi Mother," and "Sri Ramakrishna, A Prophet For the New Age." His poems have appeared in a wide variety of publications. His favorite spiritual practice is laughter and shaking (which he learned in an ashram in Bali.) He believes that lives and afterlives are a passing phenomena, but that the soul is deathless.

Neil Ellman lives and writes in the Garden State, New Jersey. His poetry appears in numerous print and online journals from "A" (Astropoetica) to "Z" (Zygote in My Coffee) and many others in between. In the afterlife, he hopes to come back as Blue-gray Gnatcatcher.

Barbara Bialick is a resident of Newton, Massachusetts who grew up in Detroit, Michigan. She has degrees from the University of Michigan and Boston University. She has published widely in newspapers, magazines, anthologies and on-line in Ibbetson Street, Pemmican, Lilith Magazine, Istanbul Literary Review, Wilderness House Literary Review, and The Boston Area Small Press and Poetry Scene, to name a few. Her chapbook TIME LEAVES (Ibbetson Street Press) can be purchased at www.lulu.com.

J.J. Steinfeld: Canadian fiction writer, poet, and play-wright J.J. Steinfeld, it is rumoured, is currently having delightful angst-ridden chats with Franz Kafka and Samuel Beckett, among other deceased literary luminaries. Before his otherworldly departure, Steinfeld published two novels, nine short story collections, and two poetry collections —including two books in 2009, Word Burials (Novel and Stories, Crossing Chaos Enigmatic Ink) and Misshapenness (Poetry, Ekstasis Editions) —along with having over forty of his one-act and full-length plays performed in Canada and the United States. According to information gathered at several recent séances, Steinfeld keeps writing away, even in his ethereal form.

Peter Rennick: Not only do I believe in the afterlife, I believe in the beforelife as well. In this lifetime I am trying to write a valentine to all things, a monumental task, for which I will have to return again and again.

Tom Clark was born in 1941 and is currently residing in an afterlife, though not perhaps the one he might have preffered. Then again, one can't have everything. His work appears most recently in the following books: *The New World* and *Trans/Versions* (Libellum); *Something in the Air* (Shearsman); *Feeling for the Ground* (BlazeVOX); and *Starlight and Shadow* (e-book: Ahadada).

Nick Doniger was raised in Connecticut and received a degree in American Studies from the University of Connecticut. He is a freelance writer, a musician, and the author of the culinary blog Sizzle Grove.

Scott Keeney is the author of *Sappho Does Hay(na)ku*. His works have lived in *BlazeVOX, Columbia Poetry Review, New York Quarterly, Poetry East,* and other journals.

Ariel Chance DeVille is sort-of Canadian; an itinerant street performer, occasional poet, mad-scientist cook and all-around kook. She reads six books a week at minimum and can walk on her hands. She is uncertain of the existence of an afterlife, but finds it vastly more intriguing to choose to accept the possibility of such a wonder than to simply discard the concept out of hand.

Anna Taborska: Anna hails from London, England. Despite being a Leo born in the middle of summer, she has always been drawn to the dark side, and loves all things horror. After a failed attempt at brainwashing in a posh girls' school and studying Experimental Psychology at Oxford University, Anna went on to gainful employment in public relations, journalism, advertising and the BBC, before throwing everything over to become a filmmaker and writer of horror stories, screenplays and poetry. Anna especially loves supernatural horror, and does not rule out the existence of ghosts.

N. A'Yara Stein is a Romani-American who currently lives on a chicory farm. She is a native of Memphis and a grant recipient of the Michigan Art Council and the Arkansas Arts Council. She's published in places such as America, The New Orleans Review, The Oxford American, California Quarterly, and Great Midwestern Quarterly, et al. Ms. Stein, an Aquarian, lives in a near Chicago with her husband and son.

Phil Gruis is the author of two chapbooks published by Finishing Line Press. His poems have appeared in many journals in the US, UK and Canada, and he's a Pushcart nominee. He lives with a brace of Newfoundlands on Kootenay Lake in British Columbia, in North Idaho and in a rolling Airstream. While thinking about the afterlife, it occurred to him that there's another scenario or two he should run by his financial advisor.

Laury Egan: My first full-length collection, Snow, Shadows, a Stranger, was issued by FootHills Publishing in 2009 and individual poems have appeared in Atlanta Review, the Ledge, Foliate Oak, The Centrifugal Eye, Boston Literary Quarterly, Emily Dickinson Awards Anthology, Ginosko, and other journals. In addition to prose writing, I am a fine arts photographer and a believer in the afterlife, persuaded by my mother's "visits." Astrological sign? Cancer Sun, Sagittarius Moon, and Aries Ascendant, a combination that keeps me very busy.

Changming Yuan, born in the year of the rooster and growing up in rural China, is a twice Pushcart nominee and author of Chansons of a Chinaman (Leaf Garden) and Politics and Poetics (LAP). Currently he teaches writing in Vancouver and has had poems appearing in nearly 250 literary publications worldwide. Believing in an afterlife, Yuan has finally found the way to become a deity after death. shhh...

Lynn Hoffman: I've been a merchant seaman, teacher, chef and cab driver. So far I've published two novels, The Bachelor's Cat and bang BANG, a novel about a woman who takes revenge on the gun lobby. I've also written The New Short Course in Wine and The Short Course in Beer. A few years ago, I started writing poetry. I was born in Brooklyn and I live in Philadelphia. My astrological sign is For Rent.

Gary Beck has spent most of his adult life as a theater director and worked as an art dealer when he couldn't earn a living in the theater. His chapbook 'Remembrance' was published by Origami Condom Press and 'The Conquest of Somalia' was published by Cervena Barva Press. A collection of his poetry 'Days of Destruction' was published by Skive Press. His poetry collection 'Expectations' was published by Rogue Scholars Press. His plays and translations of Moliere, Aristophanes and Sophocles were produced Off Broadway. His poetry has appeared in numerous literary magazines.

Greta Bolger is a writer, photographer and shopkeeper in glorious northern Michigan. Though she has no direct experience of the afterlife, she imagines it's a pretty big place. Until the time comes to find out, she'll continue to visit mediums, go to countries that celebrate the Day of the Dead, and publish her writing in print and online journals, which in the past have included Thema, The Chimaera, Eclectica, Raven Chronicles, Literary Bohemian, Juice Box, Third Coast and others.

Mary Belardi Erickson originated from Passaic, New Jersey, youthfully thrived in rural West Concord, Minnesota, and now writes poetry at the end of a long lane north of Kerkhoven, Minnesota. She is nominated for Dancz Books Best of the Web 2010 and received 2nd Place, 2009 Numinous Magazine Poetry Prize. Mary is published in a variety of online and print magazines.

Antonia Clark lives in Vermont, where she works as a medical writer and editor. Her short stories and poems have appeared in numerous print and online journals, including The 2River View, The Missouri Review, The Pedestal Magazine, Rattle, and Stirring, and she is currently co-administrator of an online poetry forum, The Waters. She loves French food and wine and plays French café music on a sparkly purple accordion. Toni would love to find out that there's an afterlife, but it doesn't look good, so she's making the most of this one.

Lisken Van Pelt Dus is a poet, teacher, and martial artist living in western Massachusetts. She is a Gemini, raised in England, the US, and Mexico, so she is accustomed to crossing borders and living with multiple consciousnesses. Her work can be found in Conduit, Main Street Rag, The South Carolina Review, upstreet, and other journals and anthologies, and has earned awards from The Comstock Review and Atlanta Review. Her chapbook, Everywhere at Once, was published by Pudding House Press in 2009.

CJ Clayton Dippolito: Is pursuing a Masters of Fine Arts in the Northeast Ohio Consortium at Youngstown State University with work published in Ruminate, Rubbertop Review, Gloom Cupboard and forthcoming in Penguin Review and Scifaikuest.

Karen Neuberg: This poem is an expansion of something I saw when my mother was dying. A few hours before she actually died—she was in and out of consciousness—she lifted her arms and hands and they began moving, as though trying to reach/touch what her open eyes were seeing beyond what we could see. She seemed to be listening and then would nod her head and softly say yes, yes. It was easy to think she was being coached by all the many family and friends who died before her—they were guiding her and encouraging her on how to pass over. They were telling her not to be afraid. They were greeting her. If I believe in an afterlife, it is more like that of a soul, an energy, leaving the body at death and (re)joining a larger energy.

Acknowledgements

I absolutely would not be able to produce any kind of finished product without the help of dozens of people. It is my truest blessing to be surrounded by the most talented, loving people I could ever hope to know. Those people include but are by no means limited to: Jocelyn Sedlor, who typeset this book; Sarah Autum, Andi Pasco, Jaret, and Bart who mastered the soundtrack and Jon Siemasko for coordinating all of the music (and for always being a great friend). Tina Mingolello, my Mother, who does more for me than I could put into words and who's expertise in design is truly appreciated. All of the poets who contributed to this project. John Mingolello, my Father, who offered much calming advice in the heat of decision making and who also houses this press; Bill and Lexi at The Owl Shop Cigar Lounge in New Haven, CT for letting me have a photo shoot inside their cozy establishment during happy hour. Serge for making me dinner and letting me work at his house when I needed a fresh environment to write in. Sarah Sartarelli, who's prophetic dream of holding the finished book in her hands gave me reason to relax and have faith and for being my very beautiful model and dear friend; Scott Keeney, the poet responsible for making Sephyrus Press real, for always supporting my wacky ideas and encouraging me to keep writing, learning and living. Byron, Frank and Brian Lipofsky for helping to edit submissions, Bill Keckler for spreading the word and keeping me laughing and inspired and, of course, Jesus (thanks for having my back;) Kathy LaLonde, my teacher; Jennifer Mingolello, my sister, who knows how to keep me happily caffienated and surrounded by beauty. A special thanks to P. A. Levy for sharing the title of his poem with the book.

www.ingramcontent.com/pod-product-compliance
Lightning Source LLC
Chambersburg PA
CBHW040325300426
44112CB00021B/2878